SAFETY CHECK

HYGIENE AND HEALTH

Written by
Valerie
Harvey

KidHaven
PUBLISHING

Published in 2027 by
KidHaven Publishing, an Imprint of Greenhaven Publishing, LLC
2544 Clinton St., Buffalo, NY 14224

Written by: Valerie Harvey
Edited by: Noah Leatherland
Designed by: Jasmine Pointer

Cataloging-in-Publication Data
Names: Harvey, Valerie.
Title: Hygiene and health / Valerie Harvey.
Description: Buffalo, NY : KidHaven Publishing, 2027. | Series: Safety check | Includes glossary and index.
Identifiers: ISBN 9781534570733 (pbk.) | ISBN 9781534570740 (library bound) | ISBN 9781534570757 (ebook)
Subjects: LCSH: Hygiene--Juvenile literature. | Health--Juvenile literature. | Health attitudes--Juvenile literature.
Classification: LCC RA777.H378 2027 | DDC 613--dc23

Printed in the United States

CPSIA compliance information: Batch #CS27KH: For further information contact Greenhaven Publishing LLC at 1-844-317-7404.

Please visit our website, www.greenhavenpublishing.com. For a free color catalog of all our high-quality books, call toll free 1-844-317-7404 or fax 1-844-317-7405.

Find us on

Image Credits:
Cover - Drazen Zigic, Fast_Cyclone. 4-5 - Prostock-studio, PeopleImages. 6-7 - sdecoret, PeopleImages, Ind_studio. 8-9 - Nastyaofly, Technicsorn Stocker, inewsfoto. 10-11 - PeopleImages, Mark Rademaker. 12-13 - Pixel-Shot, Neo Creatives, Yuliya D'yakova. 14-15 - Roman Samborskyi, Pixel-Shot, fledermausstudio, Jaimogal. 16-17 - Aaaarianne, Ilike, Sign Master Pro. 18-19 - BAZA Production, gentle studio, Prostock-studio. 20-21 - Chirtsova Natalia, PeopleImages, Pure Icons. 22-23 - Krakenimages.com, BearFotos, Elsa Nur Afiana.

All images courtesy of Shutterstock.com, unless otherwise stated.

CONTENTS

Words that look like <u>this</u> can be found in the glossary on page 24.

WHAT IS HEALTH AND HYGIENE?

Health and hygiene are all about taking care of your body every day. Keeping clean helps you stay safe from the germs that make you sick. Simple things such as washing your hands, brushing your teeth, and wearing clean clothes make a big difference.

Taking care of your body helps you play, learn, and grow. You deserve to feel healthy, happy, and full of energy!

GET GERMS GONE

Being clean gives you superstrength against germs! Germs are tiny living things our eyes can't see. They can make you sick. Keeping your body and the things you use every day clean helps stop germs from spreading.

Germs can spread when you touch things.

Washing your hands, wiping surfaces clean, and cleaning your space are great ways to be hygienic. When you stay clean, you take charge of your own well-being. That's pretty amazing!

Cleaning surfaces gets rid of germs.

CLEAN HANDS, HEALTHY BODY

Your hands touch many things every day. This means that they also pick up lots of germs. Washing your hands with warm water and soap helps get rid of the germs.

Try singing a short song while you scrub to make it fun!

Clean hands help keep your whole body healthy. It is especially important to wash them before eating and after playing outside, using the bathroom, and blowing your nose. Clean hands are cool hands!

Remember that you can't always see if your hands are dirty.

BRILLIANT SMILES

Caring for your teeth helps get rid of any bad bacteria in your mouth. Use a little toothpaste and brush gently for 2 minutes, twice a day. Make sure you get every tooth!

Bacteria can damage your teeth and give you bad breath!

Visiting the dentist helps keep your teeth strong too. Dentists check to see if everything in your mouth is healthy and clean. Clean teeth help you eat, talk, and smile without any pain.

Brushing your teeth gives you a bright smile!

BATH TIME

Bath time is a great way to wash away sweat, dirt, and germs from your skin. Warm water and gentle soap help get your body clean.

Don't forget to wash behind your ears, between your toes, and under your arms. Feeling clean helps you feel comfortable, confident, and ready for anything.

CLEAN CLOTHES

Wearing clean clothes helps keep your skin healthy and stops germs from spreading. Clothes collect dirt, sweat, and smells from all your adventures. So, changing your clothes every day is a smart habit.

Clean clothes feel comfy and cozy. They help you feel ready for school, play, or rest. When you care for your clothes, you're caring for yourself too!

Ask a trusted adult if you can help with the laundry.

FOOD FUEL

Eating a rainbow of foods—including many different colors—helps keep your body strong and healthy. Eating enough food fuels your body with the energy it needs to run, jump, learn, and grow.

Help your parents or guardians wash fruits and vegetables to remove any germs or dirt before you eat. Making sure your food is fresh and clean before eating keeps your stomach safe and happy.

SUPER SLEEP

Sleep is one of your body's best helpers. When you sleep, your body rests, repairs, and gets ready for a brand-new day. Good sleep keeps your brain working well too. Feeling rested can help you in school.

If you have trouble falling asleep, a cozy bedtime routine—such as taking a bath, brushing your teeth, and putting on clean pajamas—can help you drift off more easily.

WHEN YOU'RE FEELING SICK

Everyone feels sick sometimes, and that's OK. If you feel sick, tell an adult right away. Resting, drinking enough water, and seeing a doctor can help your body fight off illnesses.

Try to cover coughs and sneezes with your elbow, or catch a sneeze in a tissue and throw it away. This stops germs from spreading and helps keep others safe.

SAFETY STARS

You've learned so much about keeping your body healthy and hygienic. Being a Safety Star means using these habits every day—washing your hands, brushing your teeth, eating enough, and getting good sleep.

Can you be a Safety Star?

You can even share what you know with your friends to help them stay healthy too. When you take care of yourself, you shine brightly and help make the world a better place!

GLOSSARY

bacteria tiny living things, too small to see, that can cause diseases

energy the power that makes living things able to move and live

habit something someone does often, usually the same way every time

hygiene keeping the body and surroundings clean

range different types

sweat liquid that comes out of the skin when someone is hot to cool them down

well-being feeling good in the body and mind

INDEX